21
ALLEGED MISTAKES
IN THE KING JAMES BIBLE

FOR EXAMPLE:
Conies, Brass and Easter

Dr. Jack A. Moorman

Printed in the United States of America

ISBN 978-1-7376384-2-1

All Scripture quotes are from the King James Bible except those verses compared and then the source is identified.

This work was originally published as "Conies, Brass, and Easter in 2010. We are republishing it in 2021 as 21 Alleged Mistakes in the King James Bible.

Published November 2021

Address All Inquiries To:
The Old Paths Publications
142 Gold flume Way
Cleveland, GA 30528

Formatted by **TOP**:
The **O**ld **P**aths Publications, Inc.
Directors: H. D. & Patricia Williams
142 Gold Flume Way
Cleveland, GA 30528
Web: www.theoldpathspublications.com
Email: TOP@theoldpathspublications.com
Jeremiah 6:16

2.0

DEDICATION

Dr. Jack A. Moorman has gone on to his reward, so as publisher of this work, which was originally printed many years ago, but not published, I am going to speak for this dear friend. I know Brother Jack would want this work to be dedicated to his one and only wife, Dot Moorman, whom he loved with all his heart. So, Sister Dot, I have spoken for your precious husband who now walks with Jesus on the streets of gold, talking with the saints through the ages.

Dr. J. A. Moorman and his wife, Dot, 2017

TABLE OF CONTENTS

INTRODUCTION

The practice of publicly "correcting" the Standard English Bible, the Authorized Version, is probably the quickest way to undermine faith. When conservative pastors and teachers tell their people "a better rendering would be, "a more accurate translation is," "this is an unfortunate translation," "the original would better be expressed as," they are starting a chain reaction of unbelief more damaging than that caused by attacks of modernism. They are in effect saying: "God has not preserved His Word," "The Standard Bible is sullied with error." "The focus of authority has shifted from the Scriptures themselves to the teacher." Reverent exposition of the text and translation is one thing, "correction" is quite another!

But are there not justifiable reasons for "occasional" correction of the KJV? A survey of modern preaching, commentaries, Study Bibles, helps, etc., shows that there is nothing "occasional" about it! Once the practice is begun, resistance to further alteration weakens, and there is little which is not affected. Sitting under such a ministry, God's people soon find their Bible to be "in tatters."

When a Version has been a Standard for nearly 400 years, has been the measuring rod against which all others are judged, has resulted in many millions receiving Christ as Savior, has been the impetus in sending missionaries to the ends of the earth, and has spawned a world of supplemental literature - then we are dealing with a work of God! To say the least, such a Bible should be treated with the greatest respect.

If the experience of a considerable number of fundamental/evangelical leaders is anything to go by; to publicly go on record in criticizing the Authorized Version, doesn't seem to have a very happy aftermath. There is often a loss of authority in their ministry. The pulpit power Is not what it once was. They seem to find themselves on unstable and vulnerable ground. And more than a few have crashed completely and are no longer in the ministry!

THREE AREAS OF CRITICISM

1. Criticisms that are common to the Bible generally: For example, the so-called "contradictions," the reigns of the kings, etc. Without any attempt to alter the AV, completely sound answers have been given to this kind of "problem" passage. We will not be dealing with these here.

2. Criticisms which have to do with the underlying text of the Authorized Version: For example, Mark 16, John 8, 1 John 5:7, Acts 8:37, etc. Here too, substantial evidence has been brought forward which testifies to the trustworthiness of the Received Text. The present author has prepared "Manuscript Digests" which demonstrates support for a large number of passages.

"When the KJV Departs from the Majority Text" and "Early Manuscripts, Church Fathers and the Authorized Version" available from: The Old Paths Publications here: http://theoldpathspublications.com/Pages/Authors/Moorman.htm#Manuscripts

3. Criticisms directed at the English of the Authorized Version: It is this third area that we now look at, and will examine the twenty-one most frequent charges of translation error. Of course, there are other passages which might be cited, but these are the ones posing the "biggest problem." If they can be satisfactorily answered, there shouldn't be much problem with any others. The "knots" in the Bible test the heart and motives and tell a true story about a person's devotion to Scripture. When one chips away at the Standard Bible, he should be asked: "How hard did you try to get an answer?"

CHAPTER 1

BORROWED AND LENT, OR ASKED AND GAVE

ALLEGED MISTAKE: Not only does the AV translation depart from the usual meaning of the Hebrew, shaal; but it implies a certain amount of dishonesty on behalf of the Israelites. Both the Septuagint and Vulgate have 'ask', while Luther's German renders it 'demand.'

> *Exodus 3:21,22.And I will give this people favour in the sight of the Egyptians: and it shall come to pass, that, when ye go, ye shall I not go empty: [22] But every woman shall I **borrow** (shaal) of her neighbour, and of her that sojourneth in her house, jewels of silver, and jewels of gold, and raiment: and ye shall put them upon your sons, and upon your daughters; and ye shall **spoil** the Egyptians (*
>
> *Exodus 11:1 And the LORD said unto Moses, Yet will I bring one plague more upon Pharaoh, and upon Egypt; afterwards he will let you go hence: when he shall let you go, he shall surely thrust you out hence altogether. **2** Speak now in the ears of the people, and let every man **borrow** (shaal) of his neighbour, and every woman of her neighbour, jewels of silver, and jewels of gold. **3** And the LORD gave the people favour in the sight of the Egyptians. Moreover the man Moses was very great in the land of Egypt, in the sight of Pharaoh's servants, and in the sight of the people.*
>
> ***Exodus 12:33** And the Egyptians were urgent upon the people, that they might send*

> *them out of the land in haste; for they said, We be all dead men.* ***34*** *And the people took their dough before it was leavened, their kneading troughs being bound up in their clothes upon their shoulders.* ***35*** *And the children of Israel did according to the word of Moses; and they* ***borrowed*** *(shaal) of the Egyptians jewels of silver, and jewels of gold, and raiment:* ***36*** *And the LORD gave the people favour in the sight of the Egyptians, so that they* ***lent*** *(shaal) unto them such things as they required. And they* ***spoiled*** *the Egyptians.*

ANSWER: The initial instructions concerning the people "borrowing," and also how Pharoah was to be first approached, are given in the same context (3:18-22). Pharoah was only to be told about a <u>three days journey</u> (3:18; 5:3). When the Israelites first mentioned the matter of "borrowing" to their masters, they themselves may not have realized they were leaving Egypt for good. Moses was told the full extent of the Exodus in 3:8, the elders in 3:16 and 4:29; but the first clear indication of the people being so told is not until 6:6-9.

> When the Orientals go to their sacred festivals they always put on their <u>best jewels</u>. The Israelites themselves thought they were only going three days' journey to hold a feast unto the Lord, and in these circumstances it would be easy for them to borrow what was necessary for a sacred festival (Jameson, Fausset, and Brown on Exodus 12:35).

In a reference to "Studies in Oriental Social Life", pp 330-31, by H.C. Trumbull ; Merrill Unger writes:

> A persistent ancient Near East tradition, experienced by those who have servants, Is that the servants **borrow** from their employers in addition to receiving their wages. The coveted articles they get are called a "gift." Neither dishonesty nor unfairness is implied (Unger's Commentary on the Old Testament, Moody Press, Vol. I, p. 108, emphasis mine).·

This was the means by which God in judgment "spoiled" the Egyptians, compensated His people for the long years of slavery, and fulfilled the prophecy given to Abraham

> *And also that nation, whom they shall serve, will I judge: and afterward shall they come out with great substance (Genesis 15:14).*

Though the overriding meaning of shaal is "ask," and is so rendered 88 times in the AV (Young's Concordance); it is, nevertheless, capable of a number of other meanings including "enquire" - 22 times. The "Analytical Hebrew and Chaldee Lexicon" lists among its possible meanings - "To ask as a loan."

Notice two other places where <u>shaal</u> clearly means, and is translated "borrow."

> *And If a man **borrow** aught of his neighbour and it be hurt, or die, the owner thereof being not with it, he shall surely make it good (Ex. 22:14).*

> *Then he said, Go, borrow (shaal) thee vessels abroad of all thy neighbours, even empty vessels; borrow (maat) not a few (2 Kings 4:3).*

There is the further truth that all the "great substance" which the Israelites brought out of

Egypt was ultimately from God. For the first time in their history they were entrusted with material wealth. But it was "on loan," and tragically they did give it all back. In the captivities they lost everything. But even prior to that, Egypt received back some of what she had "lent"!

> *So Shishak king of Egypt came up against Jerusalem, and took away the treasures of the house of the LORD, and the treasures of the king's house; he took all :he carried away also the shields of gold which Solomon had made (2 Chronicles:12:9),*

CHAPTER 2

BRASS, OR BRONZE

ALLEGED MISTAKE: "The AV translators confused brass with bronze. The process for making brass (melting copper with zinc) was unknown in Old Testament times. Whereas bronze smelting (copper with tin) was widespread at a very early age."

> *...Tubal-cain, an instructor of every artificer in **brass** and iron (Gen. 4:22).*
>
> *thou shalt overlay it with **brass** (Ex. 27:2).*
>
> *Thou shalt also make a laver of **brass** (Ex. 30:18).*
>
> *...out of whose hills thou mayest dig **brass** (Deut, 8:9).*
>
> *he cast two pillars of **brass** (I Kings 7:15).*
>
> *he made two chapiters of molten **brass** (I Kings 7:16).*
>
> *...and all these vessels which Hiram made to King Solomon for the house of the LORD, were of **bright brass**. In the plain of Jordan did the king cast them, in the clay ground (I Kings 7:45,46).*
>
> *Iron is taken out of the earth, and **brass** is molten out of the stone (Job 28:2).*

ANSWER: It is not impossible that the Hebrews had some zinc mixed in with their copper. Note the "bright brass" of (1 Kings 7:45, 46)

The World Book Encyclopedia says:

> Some historians believe people made the first brass accidently by melting copper ore that also contained a small amount of zinc. Brass was made on the island of Rhodes as early as 500 B.C. The ancient Romans were the first to make extensive use of brass, shortly before the beginning of the Christian Era. They made a variety of brass objects, Including coins, kettles and ornaments. They made brass by melting zinc ores with copper.

The fact remains, however, that what we now call bronze and not brass was the chief alloy of the ancient world, but it was not always called this in English! Until more recent times, "brass" was the general term used for copper based alloys, whether with zinc or tin. The word "bronze" was first introduced into the English language (from the Italian "bronzo") during the 16th century, but did not displace the use of "brass" as the term for both until well into the 19th century.* Therefore, while the term may need to be explained today, the AV translators were quite correct in their choice of the word which had long-standing usage both before and after 1611."

*See: "The Oxford Dictionary of English Etymology," "The Etymological Dictionary" by W.W. Skeat, and the Oxford English Dictionary (unabridged).

CHAPTER 3

COAT OF MANY COLOURS, OR TUNIC

ALLEGED MISTAKE: "A better rendering would be 'long tunic' or one of several other translations. The Hebrew word passim (occurs five times) has at its root the idea: to expand, extend, extremities. Hence, it is a long robe with long sleeves."

> *Now Israel loved Joseph more than all his children because he was the son of his old age: and he made him a* ***coat of many colours*** *(Gen, 37:3),*
>
> *they stripped Joseph out of his coat, his* ***coat of many colours*** *that was on him (37:23).*
>
> *And they sent the* ***coat of many colours****, and they brought it to their father... (37:32).*
>
> *And she had a* ***garment of divers colours*** *upon her: for with such robes were the king's daughters that were virgins apparelled,...And Tamar put ashes on her head and rent her* ***garment of divers colours*** *that was on her (2 Sam. 13:18,19),*

ANSWER: In Bible times there was certainly nothing remarkable about a long garment with long sleeves! The Hebrew word means more. Young's Concordance interprets it as "pieces," "ends," "extremities." Editions of the AV have "pieces" in the margin. Today we speak of a "remnant" of cloth or material.

The JFB Commentary says:

> Gesenius defines it, a tunic reaching to the palms of the hands and soles of the feet . . .But the word signifies a piece as well as the palm of the hand; and hence the phrase Is usually rendered "a coat of pieces of various colours" . . it was formed in those early days by sewing together patches of coloured cloth, and considered a dress of distinction (Judges 5:30, 2 Sam. 13:18).

This latter is the view of the Targum of Onkelos (2nd century B.C.), the Talmud, Septuagint, and Jerome's Vulgate. Itis the view of Luther, Tyndale and the other European Versions of the Reformation. A number of the modern versions translates passim virtually as the AV, including the NASV and NIV. Quoting from Thornley Smith (Joseph and His Times, p. 12) Peter Ruckman says that the coat of many colours "is illustrated in Egyptian inscriptions where Semitic rulers come in to Pharoah. They are clothed in a patch-work quilt-type of garment that consists of different pieces of cloth, each one a different colour sewed together" (The Christian's Handbook of Biblical Scholarship, 1988, p. 339).

CHAPTER 4

CONIES, OR ROCK BADGERS

ALLEGED MISTAKE: "The AV 'Coney' (older English for Rabbit, cf. 'Coney Island') is certainly an error! Rabbits do not chew the cud, nor do they live in the rocks, nor in Palestine. Much the same must be said for the translation, 'Hare'! Though they are found in Israel, yet they do not chew the cud. Clearly the Rock Badger is meant for the 'Coney', and we are not certain which animal is intended for 'Hare' (See NIV and New Scofield Bible."

> *And the **coney**, because he cheweth the cud, but divideth not the hoof; he is unclean unto you. And the **hare**, because he cheweth the cud, but divideth not the hoof; he is unclean unto you (Lev. 11: 5,6).*
>
> *Nevertheless these ye shall not eat of them that chew the cud, or of them that divide the cloven hoof; as the camel, and the **hare**, and the **coney** for they chew the cud, but divide not the hoof (Deut. 14: 7).*
>
> *The high hills are a refuge for the wild goats; and the rocks for the **conies** (Psa. 104:18).*
>
> *The **conies** are but a feeble folk, yet make they their houses in the rocks (Deut. 30:26).*

The Hebrew word for Coney is shaphan. And that for Hare is arnebeth.

ANSWER: While neither animal is a true ruminant, they do rechew their food, and so in that sense "chew the cud." Rechewlng was accepted in this sense by the Hebrews.

Dake's Bible says of the hare:

> After first nibbling and partially chewing its food, the hare deposits some in its cheeks to be chewed a second time more fully before swallowing. This is spoken of as "chewing the cud" (See Lev. 11: 6).

In fact, the rock badger is not a ruminant either! It chews the cud only in the sense that a rabbit does.

As for their location, the hare is found in Palestine today and there is reason to believe that in Bible times the rabbit was also. Rabbits proliferated in North Africa and would easily have spread to Israel.

This Is the opinion of C.D. Ginsburg:

> The coney... is the meaning of the Hebrew expression shaphan according to the definition of those who had to explain and administer this law at the time of Christ. As these interpreters lived in Palestine, where they saw the animals in question, the objection that the rabbit Is not indigenous in Palestine falls to the ground (Ellicott's Commentary on Leviticus 11: 5).

As for rabbits not living in rocky places: What about those known as desert cottontails and mountain cottontails living In North America?

"Rabbit" is the translation of the Greek dasupoda in the Bagster "Septuagint, Greek and English Old Testament."

CHAPTER 5

CREATURE, OR CREATION

ALLEGED MISTAKE: "1n a number of instances (especially Romans 8) the better rendering for 'creature' would be 'creation.'"

*Go ye into all the world, and preach the gospel to every **creature** (ktisis), (Mark 16:15)•*

*...and served the **creature** (ktisis) more than the Creator (Rom. 1 :25).*

*For the earnest expectation of the **creature** (ktisis) waiteth for the manifestation of the sons of God. For the **creature** (ktisis) was made subject to vanity, not willingly, but by reason of him who hath subjected the same in hope, because the **creature** (ktisis) itself also shall be delivered from the bondage of corruption into the glorious liberty of the children of God. (Romans 8:19-2l).*

*Nor-height, nor depth, nor any other **creature** (ktisis), shall be able· to separate us... (Rom. 8:39).*

*Therefore, if any man be in Christ, he Is a new **creature** (ktisis) "2 Corinthians. 5:17),*

*For in Christ Jesus neither circumcision availeth anything, nor uncircumcision, but a new **creature** (ktisis), Gal. 6:15).*

*Who is the image of the invisible God, the firstborn of every **creature** (ktisis) Col. 1:15).*

*...the gospel...which was preached to every **creature** (ktisis) which is under heaven (Col. 1:23).*

*Neither is there any **creature** (ktisis) that is not manifest in his sight (Hebrews 4:15).*

*But from the beginning of the **creation** (ktisis) God made .them male and female (Mark 10: 6).*

*...such as was not from the beginning of the **creation** (ktisis) Mark 13:19).*

*For the invisible things of him from the **creation** (ktisis) of the world are clearly seen (Rom. 1:20).*

*For we know that the whole **creation** (ktisis) groaneth and travaileth in pain together until now (Rom. 8:22).*

*...all things continue as they were from the beginning of the **creation** (ktisis) (2 Pet. 3:4)*

*...the beginning of the **creation** (ktisis) (Rev. 3:14)*

ANSWER: The above shows clearly how the Authorized Version distinguishes between "creature" and "creation" in translating the single Greek word ktisis. In the one place it is the "creation" event itself, in the other the "creature" which springs from that event. The only instance where "creation" is not used of the event is Romans 8:22. Here, "whole creation" means "creature" in the collective sense.

The use of "creature" in Romans 8 may at first seem a little strange to twentieth century ears. Yet it is in conformity with long-standing usage, and accurately distinguishes between the act of creating (which is not the issue under discussion in Romans 8) andthe offspring of that act having been ravaged by sin (the subject of Romans 8).

This distinction becomes confused in the Modern Versions.

CHAPTER 6

DAMNATION, OR CONDEMNATION

ALLEGED MISTAKE: "In a number of passages, the AV 'damnation' is too strong! It should rather be 'condemnation' or 'judgment!'"

> *Whosoever therefore resisteth the power, resisteth the ordinance of God: and they that resist shall receive to themselves* ***damnation*** *(krima) (Rom. 13:2).*
>
> *And he that doubteth is* ***damned*** *(katakrino) if he eat, because he eateth not of faith: for whatsoever is not of faith is sin (Rom. 14:23).*
>
> *For he that eateth and drlnketh unworthily, eateth and drinketh* ***damnation*** *(krima) to himself, not discerning the Lord's body (1 Cor. 11:29).*
>
> *But the younger widows refuse: for when they have begun to wax wanton against Christ, they will marry; Having* ***damnation*** *(krlma), because they have cast off their first faith (I Tim. 5: 11,12).*

ANSWER: The Greek words can mean either the pronouncement and execution of the sentence, or the process of judging which leads to the sentence (see Vine's "Expository Dictionary"). In the former case the translation would usually be "damnation" or "condemnation," in the latter, "judgment." At times both thoughts may be combined. In the above passages, however, it is the verdict upon, and the state of the person under sentence which is in view, rather than the judging process leading to such a verdict. Therefore, the AV is correct in not using "judgment" in these passages.

As for the other two words, there is not a great deal of difference between "damnation" and "condemnation." As "damn" comes from the Latin damnare, so "condemn" does also, i.e. con (either to intensify, or meaning "together") - damnare, or literally "condamn." In our usage today the thought of eternal doom is more prominent in damnation than condemnation. Yet, in the history of the word, this was not always the case.

Charles Hodge, In his comments on 1 Cor. 11:29, says:

> The word damnation, used in our version, originally and properly means simply condemnation, and not hopeless and final perdition, which is its modern and popular sense (The First Epistle to the Corinthians, Banner of Truth Trust, p 232).

This is confirmed by the Oxford Unabridged Dictionary where six categories of meaning are given for the word "damn."

> +I. To pronounce adverse judgment (1382). To condemn to a particular penalty or fate (1300).
>
> +2 To adjudge and pronounce a thing to be bad (1385).
>
> 3. To bring condemnation upon (1477).
>
> 4. To (the theological meaning) doom to eternal punishment in the world to come (1325).

5. Used profanely (1431).

6. To imprecate (1624).

The "+" indicates that this particular usage is now archaic. The dates are those of works of literature where the word was first used in this way.

Therefore, in 1611 it was correct to use damnation both for eternal doom and also for lesser judgments; but in time this latter ceased to be used. However, in the four passages we are looking at, it would be unwise to quickly assume that the meaning is to be limited to this lesser usage. The errors of conduct given here are symptomatic of things far deeper! They are characteristic of that which <u>does</u> lead to <u>eternal</u> damnation. In each case the fault is paralleled with the more basic sin which underlies it.

Resisting the ordinance of God (Rom. 13:2).

Whatsoever is not of faith is sin (Rom. 14:23).

Not discerning the Lord's body (1 Cor. 11:29).

Have cast off their first faith (1 Tim. 5:11,12).

A man doesn't go to hell merely because he disobeyed the government. But resisting government is a mark of those who are a rebel against "the ordinance of God." All such rebels are <u>damned</u>.

A man eats meat which has been previously used in idolatrous sacrifice (Rom. 14). He is uncertain as to whether such eating constitutes idol worship, yet he goes on knowing this to be a real possibility. That man "is <u>damned</u> if he eat."

Faith cannot "halt" (1 Kings 18:21) between Christ and an idol (cf. 1 Cor. 10:2I).

The symptom is an inappropriate partaking of the Lord's Supper, but underneath lies "not discerning the Lord's body." A careless attitude toward Christ's Person and Work <u>damns</u> the soul.

Widows can remarry "in the Lord" (1 Cor. 7:39). But, the case in 1 Timothy 5 involves those who are "dead while they live" and who "cast off their first faith." Such a one <u>has damnation</u>.

Therefore, it is right to believe that the AV translators were providentially guided to use the word which fully covers both the temporal and the eternal aspects of the word.

CHAPTER 7

DEVILS, OR DEMONS

ALLEGED MISTAKE: "There is one Devil (diabolos) and many demons (daimonion, daimon). The Authorized Version confuses this distinction by translating 'devil' for the former and 'devils' (when there is more than one) for the latter. In fact, the word "demon" is not used at all in the AV."

> *But If I cast out* ***devils*** *(daimonion) by the Spirit of God ... (Matthew 12:28).*
>
> *go thy way the* ***devil*** *(daimonion) is gone out of thy daughter (Mark 7:29).*
>
> *some shall depart from the faith, giving heed to seducing spirits, and doctrines of* ***devils*** *(daimonion) (1Timothy 4:1).*
>
> *there met him out of the tombs a man with an unclean spirit...What is thy name? And he answered, saying, My name Is Legion: for we are many...And all the* ***devils*** *(daimon) besought him, saying, Send us Into the swine...And they come to Jesus, and see him that was possessed with the* ***devil*** *(daimonizomai), sitting, and clothed, and In his right mind (Mark 5:2,9,12,15).*
>
> *Then was Jesus led up of the spirit into the wilderness to be tempted of the* ***devil*** *(diabolos) (Matthew 4:1).*
>
> *...prepared for the* ***devil*** *(diabolos) and his angels (Matt. 25:41).*
>
> *Have not I chosen you twelve, and one of you is a* ***devil*** *(diabolos) (John 6:70).*

ANSWER: Common use of the word "demon" in our language is relatively late. Its first appearance in English-was not until the 15th century (Oxford Dictionary of English Etymology). Nor did it come into common theological use until a considerable time after the publication of the King James Bible. A century after the AV, commentators such as Poole and Henry consistently use "devil" rather than "demon."

In contrast, the use of "devil" as applying to both Satan and the demons goes back to the very roots of the English language.

> ... the word has been used from the earliest times in English, as equivalent to or including Demon...in the Vulgate, as in Greek, diabolos and daimon are quite distinct; but the Gothic of Ulfilas (350 A.D.) already uses unhulpa (German unhold) to render both words, and in all the modern languages, **devil**, or its cognates, is used for diabolos ("Devil," Oxford Unabridged Dictionary).

The word as it stands in our Bible clearly distinguishes Satan from his emissaries (devils, and the devil); and yet also shows the complete kinship between them. Herein lies the reason why there was a long-standing insistence to <u>translate</u> "daimonion" or "daimon" rather than merely transliterating it as is done today. From ancient Greece and onward, demons were thought to be both bad and good! They could inspire for well-being or evil.

> Its use in classical Greek is various. In Homer, where the gods are but supernatural men, it is used Interchangeably with "god;" afterwards in

> Hesiod, when the idea of the gods had become more exalted and less familiar, the "demons" are spoken of as intermediate beings, the messengers of the gods to men ("Demon", Smith's Bible Dictionary).

Many in more "orthodox" circles didn't fare much better in their understanding of demons!

> ...they are the souls of bad men, especially the spirits of those who bore a bad character in this life. This Is the view of Philo, Josephus, and practically all of the early Christian writers (Henry C. Thiessen, Introductory Lectures in Systematic Theology, Eerdmans, 1949, p. 200, emphasis mine).

The translation "devils" banishes this foolishness, and leaves the reader in no doubt as to where their kinship lies.

CHAPTER 8

DRAGONS, OR JACKALS

ALLEGED MISTAKE: "The Authorized Version has confused tannim with tannin. The latter refers to some sort of a large sea creature; but tannim is a desert animal, probably the jackal."

> *I am a brother to **dragons** (tannlm), and a companion to owls (Job 30:29).*
>
> *Though thou hast sore broken us In the place of **dragons** (tannim), and covered us with the shadow of death (Psa, 44:19).*
>
> *And the wild beasts of the islands shall cry in their desolate houses, and **dragons** (tannim) In their pleasant palaces (Isa. 13:22).*
>
> *And thorns shall come up In her palaces...and it shall be an habitation of **dragons** (tannim), and a court for owls (Isa. 34:13).*
>
> *The beast of the field shall honour me, the **dragons** (tannim) and the owls: because I give waters in the wilderness (Isa. 43:20).*
>
> *And I will make Jerusalem heaps, and a den of **dragons** (tannim) (Jer. 9:11).*
>
> *And the wild asses did stand in the high places, they snuffed up the wind like **dragons** (tannim) (Jer. 14:6).*
>
> *And Babylon shall become heaps, a dwelling place for **dragons** (tannim) (Jer. 51:37).*
>
> *Behold, I am against thee, Pharoah King of Egypt, the great **dragon** (tannim) that lieth In*

> *the midst of the rivers which hath said, My river is mine own...But I will put hooks in thy jaws, and I will cause the fish of thy rivers to stick into thy scales (Ezek. 29:3,4).*
>
> *I will make a wailing like the* ***dragons*** *(tannim), and mourning as the owls (Micah 1: 8).*
>
> *Son of man, take up a lamentation for Pharoah King of Egypt, and say unto him, Thou art like a young lion of the nations, and thou art as a* ***whale*** *(tannim) in the seas (Ezek. 32:2).*

ANSWER: The passages in Ezekiel 29:3,4; 32:2, certainly show that tannim can and does mean a lot more than "jackals"! Both the Septuagint and Vulgate translate as the AV. The Syriac, however, seems to give a different meaning:

> The Syriac renders it by a word which according to Pococke means a "jackal" (Smith's Bible Dictionary).

Commentators and translators readily accepted Pococke's verdict and changed "dragon" to "jackal" in the eleven passages where tannim is found prior to Ezekiel. But then, of course, they ran into a problem and were forced to revert back to a translation similar to the AV "dragons."

> great monster, monster (New Scofield)
>
> great monster, monster (NIV)
>
> any large aquatic animal or crocodile, any monster of the waters or crocodile (JFB Commentary)
>
> great monster or crocodile, water monster or crocodile (Unger's Old Testament Commentary)

> No Comment! (Ryrie Study Bible)

After repeatedly telling us that it ought to be "jackal," we cannot blame Ryrie for his silence on the Ezekiel passages. It is just too much to ask a jackal to suddenly become a sea monster! Tannim could not possibly admit of such a wide variation of meaning. At the very least, it refers to the crocodile or some other dangerous creature.

> Tannim usually means the crocodile; so perhaps here (Job 30:29), its open jaws lifted towards heaven, and its noise making it seem as if it mourned over its fate (Bochart in JFB).
>
> Rather the reference (Jer. 14:6) is to the great boas and python serpents, which raise a large portion of their body up in a vertical column, ten or twelve feet high, to survey the neighbourhood above the surrounding bushes, while with open jaws they drink in the air. These giant serpents originated the widely-spread notions which typified the deluge and all destructive agents under the form of a dragon or monster serpent; hence the dragon temples, always near water, in Asia, Africa, and Britain, - e.g. at Abury, in Wiltshire: a symbol of the ark is often associated with the dragon as the preserver from the waters (JFB, quoting Kitto's Biblical Cyclopedia).
>
> Hebrew, tannim, any large aquatic animal, here (Ezek. 29:3) the crocodile, which on Roman coins is the emblem of Egypt (JFB).
>
> The tannim or tanninim are any great monsters, whether of land or sea (W.E. Vine, Expository Dictionary of Old Testament Words, Oliphants, p. 51).

The above creatures would be a fit representative of that which evokes fear, i.e. of the mythical dragon or Satan himself. As serpents represent "that old serpent which is the Devil and Satan" (Rev. 20:2); so the tannlm picture "the great dragon...the devil and Satan" (Revelation 12:9). Symbols cannot depict symbols. Therefore, as with the serpent there must be an actual creature which pictures Satan in his role as Dragon. This the tannlm does, and with these other connotations in mind is rightly translated "dragon" in the Authorized Version.

CHAPTER 9

EARRING, OR NOSE JEWEL

ALLEGED MISTAKE: "The KJV translators erred in translating nezem as 'earring' in Genesis 24:22,47. Eliezer placed a nose jewel on the face of Rebekah! The fact that the word is singular further militates against the AV translation."

> *And it came to pass, as the camels had done drinking, that the man took a* ***golden earring*** *of half a shekel weight, and two bracelets for her hands of ten shekels weight of gold (Gen. 24:22),*
>
> *...and I put the* ***earring upon her face****, and the bracelets upon her hands (Gen. 24:22).*

ANSWER: The Hebrew word nezem is found 15 times in the Old Testament. The AV translates it "earring" twelve times and "jewel" three. In this latter, twice it is used for the nose and once for the forehead. That "earring" is the characteristic meaning can be seen from Genesis 35:4 and Exodus 32:2,3 where the nezim are specifically said to be placed in the ears. The passage in Genesis does not say where on Rebekah's face the nezem was placed - ear, nose, or forehead. An earring could have several different uses as jewelry.

Reflecting, no doubt, current Jewish opinion the Septuagint and Latin Vulgate understand nezim to mean "earrings."

CHAPTER 10

EASTER, OR PASSOVER

ALLEGED MISTAKE: "A most unfortunate translation! In each of the 28 other New Testament passages the Greek 'pascha' is translated 'Passover! The same is true of the Hebrew pesach, it is always 'Passover.' Why this one exception in Acts 12:4? Further, the word 'Easter' was not used in the Christian sense until much later."

> *And because he saw it pleased the Jews, he proceeded further to take Peter also. (Then were the* ***days of unleavened bread****.) And when he had apprehended him, he put him in prison, and delivered him to four quaternions of soldiers to keep him; intending* ***after Easter*** *to bring him forth to the people (Acts·12:3,4).*

ANSWER: You may be surprised to know that the word "passover" did not even exist before William Tyndale coined it for his Version of 1526-31. His was also the first English Bible to use "Easter." Previously, the Hebrew and Greek were left untranslated. For example, in Wycliffe's Bible, which was based on the Latin, we find pask or paske.

An article which appeared in The Trinitarian Bible Society Quarterly Record states:

> When Tyndale applied his talents to the translation of the New Testament from Greek into English, he was not satisfied with the use of a completely foreign word, and decided to take

> Into account the fact that the season of the passover was known generally to English people as "Easter"...Tyndale has ester or easter fourteen times, ester-lambe eleven times, esterfest once, and paschall lambe three times.
>
> When he began his translation of the Pentateuch, he was again faced with the problem in Exodus 12:11 and twenty-one other places, and no doubt recognizing that easter in this context would be an anachronism he coined a new word, passover and used it consistently in all twenty-two places. It is, therefore, to Tyndale that our language is indebted for this meaningful and appropriate word. (date of article not known).

The English versions after Tyndale followed his example in the Old Testament and increasingly replaced "Easter" with "Passover" in the New Testament. When we come to the Authorized Version there remained but one instance of the word "Easter" - Acts 12:4.

It is precisely in this one passage that "Easter" must be used, and the translation "Passover" would have conflicted with the immediate context. In their rush to accuse the Authorized Version of error many have not taken the time to consider what the passage actually says:

> *...(Then were the days of unleavened bread,)...intending after Easter to bring him forth to the people.*

To begin with, the Passover occurred before the feast of unleavened bread, not after!

> *And in the fourteenth day of the first month is the passover of the Lord. And in the fifteenth day of this month is the feast: seven days shall unleavened bread be eaten. (Num. 28:16,17). See also Mark 14:12, I Cor. 5:7,8, etc.*

Herod put Peter in Prison during the days of unleavened bread, and therefore after the Passover. The argument that the translation "Passover" should have been used as it is intended to refer to the entire period, is ruled out by the inclusion of "these were the days of unleavened bread." Scripture does not use the word "Passover" to refer to the entire period.

Peloubet's Bible Dictionary says:

> Strictly speaking the Passover only applied to the paschal supper and the feast of unleavened bread followed (p. 486).

Therefore, as the Passover had already been observed, and the days of unleavened bread were in progress, and yet Herod was still waiting for "after pascha," we can only conclude that the word must be taken in a broader sense. History in fact does indicate a pagan and Christian interchange with the word through the translation "Easter."

A.W. Watts writes:

> The Latin and Greek word for Easter Is pascha, which Is simply a form of the Hebrew word for passover - pesach. (Easter - Its Story and Meaning, p. 36).

Thus, the word came to be associated with both Christian and pagan observance. And it was to this latter that Herod was referring.

In an excellent study, from which some of the above has been drawn, Raymond Blanton explains (in quotations from Alexander Hislop) that Easter is Isthar, the queen of heaven and goddess of spring:

> The "pascha" that Herod was waiting for was evidently the celebration of the death and resurrection of Tammuz, the Sun god. The sunrise services today are a continuation of that pagan worship.
>
> "...the great annual festival in commemoration of the death and resurrection of Tammuz, which was celebrated by alternate weeping and rejoicing and which, In many countries, was considerably later than the Christian festival, being observed in Palestine and Assyria in June. To conciliate the Pagans to nominal Christianity, Rome, pursuing its usual policy, took measures to get the Christian and Pagan festivals amalgamated, and, by complicated but skillful adjustment of the calendar, it was found no difficult matter, in general, to get Paganism and Christianity - to shake hands." (Alexander Hislop, "The Two Babylons," p. 105).

Continuing his quotation from Hislop, Blanton shows:

> The term Easter is of pagan origin -
>
> "It bears its Chaldean origin on its very forehead. Easter is nothing else than Astarte, one of the titles of Beltis, the queen of heaven" (p. 103).

> The connection between the word Easter and Tammuz is thus -
>
> The wife of Tammuz was Ishtar (Astarte), who is called Mother Nature, who being refreshed by spring rains brings life. When Tammuz died she followed him Into the underworld or realm of Eresh-Kigal, queen of the dead. In her deep grief Astarte persuaded Eresh-Kigal to allow her messenger to sprinkle Astarte and Tammuz with the water of life. By this sprinkling they had power to return Into the light of the sun for six months. After which the same cycle must be repeated.
>
> Thus, the goddess of spring or the dawn goddess is responsible for the resurrection of Tammuz. Easter is a joint worship of the two. This Satanic myth Is interwoven with the sun's cycle of vernal equanox (dawn) and autumn equanox (sunset). (From "The Flaming Torch" Jan. Feb. Mar. 1987).

Dake's Bible adds:

> Easter...Is derived from Ishtar, one of the Babylonian titles of an idol goddess, the Queen of Heaven. The Saxon goddess Eastre Is the same as the Astarte, the Syrian Venus, called Ashtoreth In the O.T. It was the worship of this woman by Israel that was such an abomination to God (1 Sam. 7:3; 1 Ki. 11:5,33; 2 Ki. 23:13; Jer. 7:18; 44:18) (p. 137 N.T.).

This was the "pascha" that Herod was waiting for before releasing Peter. As an Edomite, he and his people had a long association with Babylon and her mystery religion (cf. Gen. 14:1-4).

CHAPTER 11

GROVES, OR IMAGES

ALLEGED MISTKE: "Rather than the AV 'grove,' a better rendering of the Hebrew asherah would be 'image' (New Scofield), or 'Asheroth' (Ryrie Study Bible), or 'Asherah pole' (NIV). A grove of trees cannot be the meaning for the reason that the words: to make (1 Kings 14:15; 16:33; 2 Kings 17:16, etc.), to set up (2 Kings 17:10), to stand up (2 Chr. 33:19), and to build (1 Kings 14:23) are used of the Asherah (see Unger's Bible Dictionary)."

> *...throw down the altar of Baal that thy father hath, and cut down the grove that is by it: And build an altar unto the LORD thy God upon the top of this rock...and offer a burnt sacrifice with the wood of the* ***grove*** *which thou shalt cut down...And when the men of the city arose early in the morning, behold, the altar of Baal was cast down, and the* ***grove*** *was cut down that was by it (Judges 6:25,26,28,30).*

ANSWER: Asherah is translated "grove" by the Authorized Version in each of its 40 occurrences. This is also the way the translators of the Septuagint and Jerome's Vulgate understood the word. These early Versions would most certainly have taken into account the Jewish interpretation. Something of the Jewish view, and that actual trees are involved, can be seen in the following:

> The authors of the Mishna explained the Asherah as a tree that was worshipped,

including grapevines and pomegranate, walnut, myrtle, and willow trees, and therefore, the wood and fruit must not be used ("Asherah," The Interpreter's Dictionary of the Bible, Abingdon, 1962).

This may fit in with the prohibition given in Leviticus 19:23:

> *And when ye shall come into the land, and shall have planted all manner of trees for food, then ye shall count the fruit thereof as uncircumcised: three years shall it be as uncircumcised unto you: it shall not be eaten of.*

The closest we come in the Bible to an actual description of the Asherah is Deuteronomy 16:21. Here it is obvious that it is a grove of trees, and as such, would be planted.

> *Thou shalt not plant thee a grove of trees near unto the altar of the LORD thy God.*

That this is the primary meaning is further indicated by frequent mention of the groves being cut down (not usually "broken") and burnt. It had long been the practice in heathendom to set up an idol in a grove of trees, or to prepare a grove (whether by planting or transplanting) for an idol. This, and the fact that the phrases "make," "set up," "stand up," and "build" are used collectively of groves with other idols, explains to a large extent the use of these terms.

In most passages the grove is distinguished from the idols:

> *...because she had made an* ***idol in a grove*** *(1 Kings 15:13; 2 Chr. 15:16).*

> *...ye shall destroy their altars, and break*

> *down their images, and **cut down their groves**, and burn their graven images with fire (Deut.. 7:5).*
>
> *And ye shall overthrow their altars, and break their pillars and **burn their groves** (Deut.. 12:3).*

Less often the grove is shown to be synonymous with the idol:

> *And he set a graven **image of the grove** that he had made **in the house**...(2 Kings 21:7).*
>
> *And he **brought out the grove** from the house of the LORD...and stamped it small to powder (2 Kings 23:6).*

Even in this latter sense, all indications point to the grove being a column or columns of artificial "trees."

> A symbolical tree is often found in Assyrian inscriptions, representing the hosts of heaven (Saba), answering to Asteroth, or Astarte, the queen of heaven (JFB Commentary on Isaiah 17:7).

This concurs with what we read in 2 Kings 17:16:

> *...and made a grove, and worshipped all the host of heaven and served Baal.*•

The Asherah when used in this sense was also represented as Baal's female consort.

> Asherah was a Canaanite goddess, now well-known from the Ugaritic Literature, and the idol (or wooden column) of her was generally set up beside the altars of Baal (Unger's Bible Dictionary, p. 434).

It should be noted that these latter sources indicating the use of the Asherah in a more limited sense are from outside of Israel, e.g. "The Ugaritic Literature" (Syria), and the "Assyrian inscriptions." It was probably these northern areas which saw more of this use of the Asherah. This may explain why the Syriac Peshitta alone among the three major Old Testament Versions seems (though not always) to use the word in the restricted sense. From these areas, it is likely that the cultic Asherah worship entered Israel; but, not until a later period in her history.

> ...it appears that the cult object was not known...to the patriarchs or to the kings of the United Monarchy...(it) was adopted from neighboring peoples, perhaps under the influence of such persons as Jezebel (Interpreter's Bible Dictionary).

Jezebel, it will be remembered, was from Zidon - between Israel and Syria (1 Kings 16:31).

That a wood of trees is the more usual meaning is further demonstrated by the fact that despite its frequent mention, no cultic Asherah has ever been found - neither in or outside Israel.

> No object has been found thus far in any excavation which could be called with certainty an Asherah (Ibid).

The word is found most frequently in the plural; as such, and with but one exception, it is Asherim (masculine) rather than Asheroth (feminine), (See Hastings Dictionary of the Bible, 2nd Edition, Scribner's, 1963). This further militates against seeing it solely as a female cultic object.

As for the English word "grove," the Oxford Dictionary (unabridged) leaves us in no doubt as to what it was frequently used for:

> Groves were commonly planted by heathen peoples in honour of deities to serve as places of worship or for reception of images.

To this, Smith's Bible Dictionary adds:

> In the religions of the ancient heathen world groves play a prominent part. In the old times altars only were erected to the gods within walls, and hence trees were the first temples.

And finally in his famous "The Land and the Book," W.H. Thompson writes:

> And one other thought about these remarkable trees. This country abounds in them. We have sacred trees, and trees that are inhabited by jin, or evil spirits; and we have single trees all over the land covered with bits of rags from the garments of passing villagers, hung up as acknowledgments or as deprecatory signals and charms...These are doubtless relics of most ancient superstitions.

The Authorized Version "groves" best represents the varied facets of the case, and brings out the meaning far better than "images" or if left untranslated as "Asherah."

CHAPTER 12

HOLY GHOST, OR SPIRIT

Alleged Mistake: "With regard to the Holy Spirit, the Authorized Version is inconsistent in its translation of pneuma. Except in four instances (Luke 11:13; Eph. 1:13; 4:30; 1 Thes. 4:8), when prefixed with 'Holy' it is 'Holy Ghost!.' Elsewhere it is rendered 'Spirit.' Further, the word "Ghost" gives a wrong connotation.".

> *And it was revealed unto him by the **Holy Ghost**, that he should not see death, before he had seen the Lord's Christ, And he came by the **Spirit** Into the temple (Luke 2:26,27).*
>
> *Upon whom thou shalt see the **Spirit** descending, and remaining on him, the same is he which baptizeth with the **Holy Ghost** (John 1:33).*
>
> *But this spake he of the **Spirit**, which they that believe on him should receive for the **Holy Ghost** was not yet given (John 7:39).*
>
> *And they were all filled with the **Holy Ghost**, and began to speak with other tongues, as the **Spirit** gave them utterance (Acts 2:4).*
>
> *...and were forbidden of the **Holy Ghost** to preach the word in Asia, After they were come to Asia, they assayed to go into Bithynia: but the **Spirit** suffered them not (Acts 16:6,7).*
>
> *...no man speaking by the **Spirit** of God calleth Jesus accursed: and that no man can say that Jesus is the Lord, but by the **Holy Ghost** (1 Corinthians 12:3).*

"Holy Ghost" is found 90 times in the New Testament, the four occurrences of "Holy Spirit" are -

> *If ye then, being evil know how to give good gifts unto your children: how much more shall your* ***heavenly Father give the Holy Spirit*** *to them that ask him (Luke 11:13)?*
>
> *in whom also after that ye believed, ye were sealed with that* ***holy Spirit*** *of promise (Ephesians. l:13).*
>
> *And grieve not the* ***holy Spirit of God****, whereby ye are sealed unto the day of redemption (Eph. 4:30.,*
>
> *He therefore that despiseth, despiseth not .man, but God who hath also given unto us* ***his holy Spirit*** *(1 Thes. 4:8).*

ANSWER: When prefixed with "Holy" and presented in a singular sense - generally apart from the Father and Son - the august title of the Third Person is "The Holy Ghost." When presented in His relationships with Father and Son, the title "Spirt" is used. A survey of all the passages (see for example, "The Englishman's Greek Concordance") shows this distinction to be maintained consistently in the Authorized Version. A possible exception is His baptizing work (Matt. 3:11; Mark 1:8) where "Holy Ghost" is used in connection with the Son. Out as this is His primary and initial work on behalf of believers, we find the title used.

From this it seems apparent that throughout much of English church history, "Holy Ghost" was considered a more elevated and exalted title than

"Holy Spirit." It is certainly the more ancient of the two, as it goes back to the very roots of the English language; whereas "Holy Spirit" did not begin to be used until the 13th century (Oxford Dictionary of English Etymology).

But could there not be a deeper and providential reason for the rendering "Holy Ghost"? With the word "ghost," death and its aftermath comes immediately to mind - albeit often in a superstitious sense. Yet death does mark the word! He is the Holy Ghost and could·only·come·after a certain death had been accomplished (John 7:39; 14:26; 16:7); and bears witness to Him "that liveth, and was dead" (Rev. 1:18; Acts 4:8,10).

CHAPTER 13

HOLY THING, OR HOLY ONE

ALLEGED MISTAKE: "It is irreverent for the Authorized Version in Luke 1:35 to refer to Christ as 'that holy thing.' It should rather be 'that holy one.'"

> *Then said Mary unto the angel, How shall this be, seeing I know not a man? And the angel answered and said unto her, The Holy Ghost shall come upon thee, and the power of the Highest shall overshadow thee: therefore also that **holy thing** which shall be born of thee shall be called the Son of God (Luke 1:34,35).*

ANSWER: In the first place, to criticize the AV at this point, while at the same time embracing a modern version such as the NIV which removes N.T. names of Christ and titles of Deity in 176 places - is inconsistent to say the least!

The Greek, hagion is neuter (rather than hagios masculine) and means literally "holy thing" (see: Alfords Greek New Testament; Berry's Interlinear; The Analytical Greek N.T. etc.).It is "an expression denoting the singularity and consequent sanctity of this birth" (JFB Commentary). It harks back to the first promise of the Incarnation in Genesis 3:15. Notice here the use of the neuter pronoun in reference to Christ:

> *And I will put enmity between thee and the woman, and between thy seed and her seed; **it** shall bruise thy head, and thou shalt bruise his heel.*

Matthew Henry says of Luke 1:35 -

> The child she shall conceive is a holy thing, and therefore must not be conceived by ordinary generation, because he must not share in the common corruption and pollution of the human nature. He Is spoken of emphatically, That Holy Thing, such as never was; and he shall be called the Son of God, as the Son of the Father by eternal generation, as an indication of which he shall now be formed by the Holy Ghost In the present conception. His human nature must be so produced, as it was fit that should be which was to be taken into union with the divine nature.

Primarily, "that holy thing" refers to our Saviour's human nature which would be brought into union with His divine nature - rather than His Person as such. The translation "Holy One" confuses this distinction.

CHAPTER 14

ITALICS IN 1 JOHN 2:23

ALLEGED MISTAKE: "The AV translators were wrong to use Italic type in the second half of 1 John 2:23!"

> Whosoever denieth the Son, the same hath not the Father: ***(but) he that acknowledgeth the Son hath the Father also***.-

ANSWER: There were six basic reasons or guidelines followed by the AV translators in the use of italic type. Five were to smoothen in various ways the interchange from Hebrew and Greek into English. In the sixth, the translators are expressing that while they felt the passage was part of Scripture, yet their current sources were inconclusive. In fact, there is only one clear occurrence of this use of italic type in the entire King James Bible - 1 John 2:23 (See F.H.A. Scrivener, "The Authorized Edition of the English Bible," Cambridge Press, 1884, pp. 61ff., 254).

There was a paucity of Greek manuscript support for the passage prior to 1611. It was therefore omitted from the early printed Greek editlons – the Complutensian, Erasmus, Stephanus, and the early editions of Beza. Wycliffe, based on the Latin Vulgate, inserted the passage in his English Bible. Yet the Latin evidence at that time did not seem conclusive (nor is it strongly conclusive today). Excepting Wycliffe, it was not in the early English versions - Tyndale, Coverdale and the Geneva edition of

1560. However, The Great Bible (1539), brought the passage - italicized and within brackets – into the English text. This was followed by the Bishops, still italicized but without the brackets, in 1568. Beza included the passage in his latter Greek editions, which provided the primary basis of the AV. Since 1611, substantial Greek support for the passage has come to light, as well as from the Syriac and Coptic.

Thus the AV translators took the prudent course; they voted on the side of the passage, while at the same time acknowledging the inconclusiveness of their available evidence.

CHAPTER 15

PENNY, OR DENARIUS

ALLEGED MISTAKE: "By rendering denarius as "penny," the AV translators have left us with a completely wrong impression. How could a penny be the equivalent of a day's wage (which the denarius was)?"

> *And when he had agreed with the labourers for **a penny a day**, he sent them into his vineyard (Matt. 20:2).*
>
> *Shall we go and buy **two hundred pennyworth** of bread, and give them to eat (Mark 7:37)?*
>
> *Why was this waste of the ointment made? For it might have been sold for more than **three hundred pence**, and have been given to the poor (Mark 14:4,5).*
>
> *...he took out **two pence**, and gave them to the host, and said unto him, Take care of him; and whatsoever thou spendest more, when I come again, I will repay thee (Luke 10:35).*
>
> *A measure of wheat for **a penny**, and three measures of barley for **a penny** (Revelation 6:6).*

ANSWER: Those unfamiliar with the British system of Pounds, Shillings, and Pence (or Pennies), will be surprised to learn that prior to 1971 the penny was represented by "d." For example, 50 pence was written "50d," The "d" stood for denarius!

Based on the Roman denarius, the English penny was a silver coin Introduced during the 8th century by two little-known Anglo-Saxon kings of Kent and popularized by the powerful King Offa of Mercia. Because of the rising price of silver and the need for a greater number of coins as trade and commerce increased, the silver penny was steadily reduced in size. The pennies of Elizabeth I (1558-1603) were only about one-third the weight of those of William the Conqueror, and the metal was much debased. The first regal copper pennies were not issued until 1797 ("Coin": 1989 Year Book).

As Britain had been a colony of Rome, the British penny was a kind of lineal descendant of the Roman Denarius, which in turn had been the principal coin of the Empire during New Testament times.

> In the time of Augustus 84 denarii were struck from the pound of silver, which would make the standard weight about 60 grains (1 ounce). This Nero reduced by striking 96 from the pound which would give ·a standard weight of about 52 grains, results confirmed by the coins of the periods, which are, however, not exactly true to the standard. In Palestine, in the N,T. period, we learn from numismatic evidence that denarii must have mainly formed the silver currency. From the parable of the laborers in the vineyard it would seem that a denarius was then the ordinary pay for a day's labor {Unger's Bible Dictionary, p. 724).

For many centuries the silver penny (d) was the chief or only coin used in England. In as much as it was halved (half-penny), and quartered (farthing), shows that it was of significant value. In fact, it was even counterfeited! "The Pollard was the name given to a counterfeit penny struck in base silver and imported from Europe during the reign of Edward I (1272-1307) ("Coin").

As for its purchasing power: Around 1750, the average weekly wage for a labourer in London was a little under 10 shillings (12 pennies to a shilling), and that for a farm worker about 7 shillings (see Chambers Encyclopedia, "Wages and Salaries"). Coming down to the period before the translation of the Authorized Version, agricultural workers were given accommodation and one shilling a week. Thus, we are reasonably close to the penny a day of Matthew 20.

However, the use of "penny" in ·the AV should be seen in a broader context than the question of its value at a given time. In the 14th century, the "pennyweight" (the weight of the silver penny), became a unit of measure within the Troy system of weighing precious metals and coins.

> In the system of troy weight, the pound contains 12 ounces (as compared with 16 ounces in the avoirdupois system). The ounce equals 20 pennyweights, and the pennyweight equals 24 grains ("Troy Weight," World Book Encyclopedia).

Further, the word "penny" was something of a generic term. The Oxford Unabridged Dictionary explains:

> From the fact that the sliver penny was for many hundred years the chief or only coin In circulation, the name became to a great extent

> synonymous with “coin,” "piece," or "unit of money.”

Therefore, whatever inflation may have done to the penny since 1611, its significance as a unit of currency had long been established and this is accurately reflected in the AV translation.

CHAPTER 16

ROBBERS OF CHURCHES, OR·TEMPLES

ALLEGED MISTAKE: "The AV translation 'robbers of churches' is wrong. The Greek is hierosulos (hieron, 'a temple'; and sulao, 'to rob'). It should have been translated 'robbers of temples', i.e. heathen temples such as the Temple of Diana."

> *For ye have brought hither these men, which are neither **robbers of churches**, nor yet blasphemers of your goddess (Acts 19:37).*

ANSWER: The AV reading follows that of the earlier English Versions, including Tyndale and the Geneva. In former times the word "church" was used in a broader sense than it is now.

> It was not unusual for the writers of the Elizabethan age to apply the term which we confine to Christian buildings, to heathen temples. They would speak; e.g. of the "church" of Diana, or the "chapel" of Apollo (E.H. Plumptre, Acts, Ellicott's N.T. Commentary).

See the commentaries of Poole and Henry as an example of this.

Nevertheless, it is remarkable that in the 71 N.T. occurrences of hieron, the AV always translates it "temple," including verse 27 of this same chapter "the temple of the great goddess Diana," But here, and in Rom. 2:22 where it is also combined with sulos, "temple" does not come into the translation.

> *Thou that sayest a man should not commit adultery, dost thou commit adultery? Thou that abhorrest idols, dost thou* ***commit sacrilege****?*

In two other instances, hieros (the closely related masculine form) is found in combination -

1. hierourgeo, "to labour in sacred things" (Rom. 15:16).

> *That I should be the minister of Jesus Christ to the Gentiles,* ***ministering*** *the gospel of God...*

2. hieroprepees, "that which befits the sacred."

> *The aged women likewise, that they be in behaviour as* ***becometh holiness*** *(Titus 2:3).*

Therefore, it is not unlikely that a broader meaning is intended for hierosulos then strictly "robbers of heathen temples." Indeed; "The noun is more common than the verb for sacrilege in general. In later comedy the word is used very loosely and generally with great exaggeration as a term of abuse" (Kittel, Theological Dictionary of the New Testament). Though this silversmith's trade had fallen on hard times, no one was suggesting for a moment that Paul and his associates actually stole from the Temple of Diana. The point the town clerk made was that they were not robbers of churches, i.e. "religious robbers," in the more general sense. Paul did not enrich himself through "religion," nor were the churches, which by this time were springing up throughout Asia Minor, a source of enrichment. The KJV wording highlights what has been the chief accusation (whether justified or not) of the unconverted from that day to this: "The preacher is in it for the money!"

> *And through covetousness shall they with feigned words make merchandise of you (2 Peter 2:3).*

> *Did I make a gain of you by any of them whom I sent unto you? (2 Corinthians. 12:9)*

This, Paul most certainly did not do! Yet, ponder the wording in 2 Corinthians " -

> *Have I committed an offence In abasing myself that ye might be exalted, because I have preached to you the gospel of God freely? I **robbed other churches**, taking wages of them, to do you service (2 Corinthians. 11:7,8).*

Though there have been exceptions (c.f. Spanish Catholics plundering Aztec temples), "robbing temples" has not been a common charge laid against professed Christian leaders. But certainly, "robbing churches" is!

The KJV wording gives a long-term application for those who would "fleece the flock."

CHAPTER 17

STRAIN "AT" OR "OUT" A GNAT

ALLEGED MISTAKE: "This misprint in the King James Version has never been corrected" (Ryrie Study Bible). "All the former translations, including Tyndale, had "out" (See the Companion Bible). "The Greek word diulizontes means 'to filter or strain thoroughly or through'" (Vincent's Word Studies). "How can you strain at a gnat?"

> *Ye blind guides, which strain* ***at*** *a gnat and swallow a camel (Matthew 23:24).*

ANSWER: There were a few typographical errors in early printings of the AV. These were corrected in subsequent editions. But, there is no evidence that this reading was viewed by early editors as either a printing error or a slip by the translators themselves. Early commentators such as Poole and Henry do not mention any problem with the passage.

Two well-known 19th century commentators remark:

> It is sometimes said that the present rendering of the Authorized Version is but the perpetuation of a printer's blunder; but of this there is scarcely sufficient evidence, nor is it probable in itself (E.H. Plumptre in Ellicott's New Testament Commentary).

> ...seems not to have been a mistake, as sometimes supposed, but a deliberate alteration, meaning, "strain (out of the wine) at (the occurrence of) a gnat" (Henry Alford, The Greek New Testament).

Normally, for the word "out" we would expect to see a Greek preposition such as ek or apo, but there is none here. Further, "gnat" is singular. The Pharisees had placed all of their attention and energies upon one solitary gnat, and this at the expense of swallowing a camel! We do not have here a case of a general straining for impurities, Therefore, expositions such as the following completely miss the point:

> ...The Jews strained their wine in order not to swallow any unclean animal. Moreover, there were certain insects which bred in wine. Aristotle uses the word gnat of a worm of larva found in the sediment of some wine. "In a ride from Tangier to Tetuan I observed that a Moorish soldier who accompanied me, when he drank, always unfolded the end of his turban and placed it over the mouth of his bota, drinking through the muslin to strain out the gnats whose larve swarm in the water of that country. (Vincent's Word Studies, with citation from R.C. Trench).

There Is nothing "little" about taking usual hygienic or even ceremonial precautions as in straining out gnat larvae. But this is not the issue here. The passage as it is commonly read - one labouring, striving, "straining" over a little gnat - comes close to the intended meaning. It is not as much the method (filtering by one means or another) as it is the fanaticism and effort in getting at one insignificant gnat. When that lone creature suddenly appeared in the glass, the world stopped, while it was strained at! Only the KJV translation brings out this force.

CHAPTER 18

SYNAGOGUES, OR MEETING PLACES

ALLEGED MISTAKE: "Asaph, as King David's choir director, could not have known about synagogues at the time Psalm 74 was written. They did not exist for another 600 years. A better rendering would be 'meeting places!'" (Ryrie Study Bible)

> *Thine enemies roar in the midst of thy **congregations** (moed); they set up their ensigns for signs. A man was famous according as .he had lifted up axes upon the thick trees. But now they break down the carved work thereof at once with axes and hammers. They have cast fire into thy **sanctuary** (miqdash), they have defiled by casting down the dwelling place of thy name to the ground. They said in their hearts, Let us destroy them together: they have burned up all the **synagogues** (moed) of God In the land (Psalm 74:4-8).*

ANSWER: As synagogues were "places" where Jews "met" to hear the Law of God and pray, there is not a great deal of difference between the terms. In the more usual sense of the word, we look to the period after the Babylonian captivity for the beginning of the synagogue service, yet forerunners probably existed before. In Jehoshaphat's day (860 BC) there were gatherings to hear the Law throughout the land (2 Chr. 17:7-9), "Josephus, Philo, and later Judaism generally (Unger's Bible Dictionary) speak of the early roots of the system. The New Testament says that synagogues were "of old time."

> *For Moses of old time hath In every city them that preach him, being read In the synagogues every sabbath day (Acts 15:21).*

So it is conceivable that Psalm 74:6 could be referring to these forerunners of the post-exilic synagogues. But, the answer is to be found elsewhere! Psalm 74 Is prophetic of the long period of desolation and dispersion after Nebuchadnezzar destroyed the temple (verse 7). Thus -

> *Why hast thou cast us off forever (v 1)?*
>
> *Lift up thy feet unto the perpetual desolations (v 3),*
>
> *There Is no more any prophet; neither Is there among us any that knoweth how long (v 10).*

This can only describe "the times of the Gentiles" (Luke 21:24) when at various times "they have burned up all the synagogues of God in the land."

CHAPTER 19

THE SON OF GOD, OR A SON OF THE GODS

ALLEGED MISTAKE: "While the 'fourth person' may have been the Son of God, Nebuchadnezzar would not know this, and therefore speaks of him as 'a son of the gods! This is confirmed In verse 28 where Nebuchadnezzar acknowledges that 'God sent his angel to deliver Shadrach, Meshach, and Abednego.' Further, the Aramaic form elahin is plural, and whenever used in the Aramaic section of Daniel seems to refer to the gods of the heathen; whereas the singular elah is used for the True God." (see The New Scofield, Ryrie, NIV etc.)

> *He answered and said, Lo, I see four men loose, walking in the midst of the fire, and they have no hurt;· and the form of the fourth Is like* ***the Son of God****. Then Nebuchadnezzar came near to the mouth of the burning fiery furnace, and spoke and said, Shadrach, Meshach, and Abednego, ye servants of the* ***most high God****, come forth (Dan. 3:25,26).*

ANSWER: The Bible believer should note that as far as "contemporary scholarship" is concerned there is a tendency to find a problem with many of the prophecies, and revelations of Christ in the Old Testament!

In the passage before us, it Is not only a question of how Nebuchadnezzar could speak about "the Son of God" but how could he also speak about El Elyon (in Chaldee it is illal), "the Most High God." For verse 26 is the first instance of this title of Deity in Daniel. The answer can only be: By revelation!

As in the case of Caiaphas,

> *And one of them, named Caiaphas, being the high priest that same year, said unto them, Ye know nothing at all, Nor consider that it is expedient for us, that one man should die for the people, and that the whole nation perish not. And this spake he not of himself: but being high priest that year, he prophesied that Jesus should die for that nation (John 11:49-51).*

And the Centurion,

> *Now when the centurion, and they that were with him, watching Jesus, saw the earthquake and those things that were done, they feared greatly, saying, Truly this was the Son of God (Matt. 27: 54).*

The Scriptures promise a universal revelation of Christ,

> *That was the true Light which lighteth every man that cometh into the world (John 1:9).*

A.R. Fausset believes this to be the case concerning Nebuchadnezzar:

> Unconsciously, like Saul, Caiaphas, and Pilate, he is made to utter divine truths, the full import of which he did not himself understand (JFB_Commentary).

As for his statement in 3:28, Christ in Old Testament times was indeed the Angel of the Lord and the Messenger of the Covenant.

But the matter that is frequently overlooked is that Nebuchadnezzar had already been given a prior revelation of Christ in chapter 2!

> *But there is a God in heaven that revealeth secrets, and maketh known to the King Nebuchadnezzar what shall be in the latter days {2:28).*
>
> *Thou sawest till that **a stone** was cut out without hands, which smote the Image upon his feet...and **the stone** that smote the image became a great mountain, and filled the whole earth (2:34,35).*

There is certainly no problem with the plural "Son of elahin" in 3:25. Elahin is the Chaldee spelling of the plural Elohim. As Elohim, depending on the context, is used of the True God in the Trinity of His Being and also of false gods; so it would be with Elahln (see 6:20). In the idolatrous climate of Babylon which captive Judah found itself, the singular Elah is used in Daniel (and Ezra) as a counter to that idolatry, while Elahin is used of the false deities. But believing that Nebuchadnezzar's words in 3:25 are a revelation rather than merely a startled exclamation, Elahin/Elohim is used here in its usual sense of the true God.

There should be no doubt that it was in fact the Son of God in the fiery furnace with the three Hebrews. Whenever a singular angelic personage appears in the Old Testament, it is invariably the Preincarnate Christ. Christ had previously been in the flames of the bush speaking to Moses, and would shortly be in the lion's den with Daniel.

Note also, "the Son of God" is the reading in the Septuagint.

CHAPTER 20

THE SPIRIT ITSELF, OR HIMSELF

ALLEGED MISTAKE: "On two occasions we find 'the Spirit Itself' in the Authorized Version. The Holy Spirit Is not an 'it'! The translation should be 'himself'."

> *...but ye have received the Spirit of adoption, whereby we cry, Abba, Father. The Spirit **itself** beareth witness with our spirit, that we are the children of God (Rom. 8:15,16).*
>
> *Likewise the Spirit also helpeth our infirmities: for we know not what we should pray for as we ought; but the Spirit **itself** maketh intercession for us with groanings which cannot be uttered. And he that searcheth the hearts knoweth what is in the mind of the Spirit, because he maketh intercession for the saints according to the will of God (Rom. 8:26,27).*

ANSWER: In both instances "the Spirit itself" is the literal translation of <u>auto to pneuma</u> - itself the spirit. <u>Pneuma</u> Is neuter (rather than masculine) as is also the pronoun <u>auto</u>. Therefore, the AV translation is grammatically correct. Further, it is in accord with the fact that the Bible often stresses the <u>workings</u> of the Holy Spirit rather than His Person. Personality <u>is</u> clearly taught. Notice "he" in Romans 8:27. But the emphasis in 8:14-26 is on the influence and workings of the One whom Scripture likens to wind, fire, water, oil. Unlike Father and Son, personal names are not given to Him, nor does He appear to men as a Person in Scripture. He is the Holy Spirit! Father and Son appear on the throne in Revelation 4 and 5, but He appears as "seven lamps of fire burning before the throne, which are the seven Spirits of God" (4:5). In John 16:13 where His personality is stressed the Greek departs from the usual practice, and a masculine pronoun is used with the neuter Spirit - ekeinos to pneuma.

*When **he** the Spirit of truth is come...*

It is to be further noted, that while there was no question of their belief in the personality of the Holy Spirit, the great commentators of the past interchanged the personal and impersonal pronouns when speaking of Him.

Commenting on Romans 8:15,16, Matthew Poole (17th century) wrote:

> The Spirit of God is called the Spirit of Adoption, both because He works and effects in us, and because He testifies and assures it to us...The Spirit of adoption doth not only excite us to call upon God as our Father, but it doth ascertain and assure us that we are His children. And this it doth, not by an outward voice...but by an inward and secret suggestion...This is not the testimony of the graces and operations of the Spirit, but of the Spirit itself (quoted in "The Spirit of God," Article #20, The Trinitarian Bible Society, pp. 1,2).

This same article gives reasons why "himself" and "itself" were used interchangeably:

> The English language now has the masculine and feminine pronouns...he, him, his, (to him);

and she, her, hers, (to her). The neuter pronoun - it, it, its (to it) represents a modified form of the Old English - hit, hit, his, (to him). During the Middle English period this neuter pronoun lost its initial h and passed into standard English as - it, its, and In the 16th century there was a tendency to use his only In relation to masculine nouns, and to use thereof or of it for the neuter genitive, and in course of time the genitive or possessive it's and then Its came Into common use In relation to neuter nouns in the 17th century.

In many Instances the older form of the neuter pronoun and possessive adjective survived in the English Bible, as in Genesis 1:11 "the fruit tree yielding fruit after his kind," we would now use "its kind." It would be quite wrong to imagine that the translators here intended to invest the inanimate tree with personality by using his kind, and it would be equally wrong to assert that the translators attempted to divest the Holy Spirit of personality in Romans 8 by using the form "itself" (pp. 2,3).

CHAPTER 21

ELIZABETHAN ENGLISH, ARCHAIC WORDS, THEE AND THOU

ALLEGED MISTAKE: "Moreover, there is a decreasing number of people today who can read Elizabethan English and readily understand it" (D.A. Carson, The King James Version Debate, Baker Book House, 1979, p. 98).

"English usage has undergone profound changes since the first publication of the King James edition. This has created a growing difficulty for readers of our time" (Introduction to New King James Bible).

"Language is not static. In the three and a half centuries since that version was published some English words have become obsolete or archaic; others have altered and, in some instances, even reversed their meanings" (Introduction to the New Scofield Bible).

> *...my master left me, because three days* ***agone*** *(ago I fell sick (1 Samuel 30:13).*

> *...the same is he that heareth the word, and* ***anon*** *(immediately) with joy receiveth it (Matthew 13:20).*

> *With him will I speak mouth to mouth, even* ***apparently*** *(openly), and not in dark speeches (Numbers 12:8).*

> *Saul...****assayed*** *(attempted) to join himself*

to the disciples: but they were all afraid of him (Acts 9:26).

They have ***belied*** *(denied) the LORD, and said it is not he; neither shall evil come upon us (Jeremiah 5:12).*

And they rose up ***betimes*** *(early) in the morning (Genesis. 26:31).*

...thy speech ***bewrayeth*** *(betrays) thee (Matthew 26:73).*

...furbish the spears, and put on the ***brigandines*** *(coats of mail) (Jeremiah 46:4).*

Behold, the noise of the ***bruit*** *(report) Is come (Jeremiah 10:22).*

...for these things must first come to pass; but the end is not ***by and by*** *(immediately) (Luke 21:9).*

...we took up our ***carriages*** *(baggage that you "carry"), and went up to Jerusalem (Acts 21:15).*

Beside that which ***chapmen*** *(traders) and merchants brought (2 Chronicles 9:14).*

And old shoes and ***clouted*** *(patched, mended) upon their feet (Joshua 9:5).*

...and slew all the children that were In Bethlehem, and in all the ***coasts*** *(borders) thereof (Matthew 2:16).*

...although the enemy could not ***countervail*** *(compensate for) the King's damage (Esther 7:4).*

Let him ***eschew*** *(shun) evil, and do good; let him seek peace, and* ***ensue*** *(pursue) it (1 Peter 3:11).*

...before whose eyes Jesus Christ hath

been ***evidently*** *(openly, clearly, "with evidence") set forth, crucified among you? (Galatians 3:1)?*

Yea, the fir trees rejoice at thee…saying, Since thou art laid down, no ***feller*** *(hewer, to "fell") is come up against us (Isaiah 14:8).*

Thou shalt not go up- but ***fetch a compass*** *(make a circuit) behind them (2 Samuel 5:23).*

Stay me with ***flagons*** *(raisen cakes), comfort me with apples (Songs 2:5).*

…fowls…beasts…and none shall ***fray*** *(frighten) them away (Jeremiah 7:33).*

He that hath a ***froward*** *(crooked, wayward) heart findeth no good (Proverbs 17:20).*

And Uzziah prepared…shields, and spears, and helmets, and ***habergeons*** *(coats of mail), and bows (2 Chronicles 26:14).*

And they shall pass through It, ***hardly bestead*** *(oppressed, distressed} and hungry (Isaiah 8:21).*

Thou shalt destroy them that speak ***leasing*** *(falsehood) (Psalm 5:6).*

I purposed to come unto you, but was ***let*** *(hindered) hitherto (Rom. 1:13).*

…but have done unto him whatsoever they ***listed*** *(willed) (Matthew 17:12).*

A man that beareth false witness against his neighbour is a ***maul*** *(club), and a sword, and a sharp arrow (Proverbs 25:18).*

…praise him with stringed instruments and ***organs*** *(pipes, "mouth organs") (Psalm 150:4).*

And they wrought onyx stones enclosed in ***ouches*** *(settings) of gold (Exodus 39:6).*

*His mischief shall return upon his own head, and his violent dealing shall come down upon his own **pate** (crown of head) (Psalm 7:16).*

*And Jacob took him rods of green poplar...and **pilled** (peeled) white **strakes** (streaks) in them (Gen. 30:37).*

*Neither shall they shave their heads, nor suffer their locks to grow long; they shall only **poll** (cut) their heads (Ezekiel 44:20).*

*....in the morning shall my prayer **prevent** (come before) thee (Psalm 88:13).*

*Watch ye, stand fast in the faith, **quit you** like men (act like men) (1 Corinthians 16:13).*

*Nor **script** (small money bag or wallet) for your journey (Matthew 10:10).*

*Doth he thank that servant...I **trow** (think) not (Luke 17:9).*

*...and a **wench** (maidservant) went and told them (2 Samuel 17:17).*

*...they said one to another, it is manna: for they **wist** (knew) not what it was (Exodus 16:15).*

*And Abimelech said, I **wot** (know) not who hath done this thing (Genesis 21:26).*

*And the changeable suits of apparel, and the mantles, and the **wimples** (head coverings), and the **crisping pins** (purses) (Isaiah 3:22).*

ANSWER: These forty-four words are the ones most likely to give some difficulty to the average reader. A few others might have been mentioned, but not many.

Most of the above are used infrequently (some

only once or twice), and often the meaning can be easily seen from the context. So, where are the "profound changes" that the New KJV speaks about? This point has been greatly exaggerated. The problems with the Modern Versions are infinitely greater and more numerous than these forty-four older English words. (See the author's "Missing in Modern Bibles").

It is an evidence of God's Providence that after nearly four centuries, so little can be found to be archaic in the Authorized Version. Certainly there are "profound differences" between current and Elizabethan English. But the AV is not Elizabethan English! As a comparison will show, there is a great difference between AV English and the wordy, affectatious Elizabethan style.

Far from our Bible being a product of that day's literary style, the English language after 1611 owes its development to the Authorized Version! "The King James Version was a landmark in the development of English prose. Its elegant yet natural style had enormous influence on English-speaking writers" (World Book Encyclopedia). This partially explains why the AV is ever fresh and lucid while most else from that period is quite difficult to read.

Edward F. Hills speaks clearly on the misconception that the English of the AV is Elizabethan:

> ...the English of the King James Version is not the English of the early 17th century. To be exact, it is not a type of English that was ever spoken anywhere. It is biblical English, which

> was not used on ordinary occasions even by the translators who produced the King James Version. As H. Wheeler Robinson (1940) pointed out, one need only compare the preface written by the translators with the text of their translation to feel the difference in style.
>
> And the observations of W.A. Irwln (1952) are to the same purport. The King James Version, he reminds us, owes its merit, not to 17th-century English - which was very different - but to Its faithful translation of the original. Its style is that of the Hebrew and of the New Testament Greek. Even In their use of thee and thou the translators were not following 17th century English usage but biblical usage, for at the time these translators were doing their work these singular forms had already been replaced by the plural you in polite conversation (The King James Version Defended, Des Moines: Christian Research Press, 1984, pp. 218).

Taking up Hill's point about the use of thee and thou, a current modern version says the following in its Introduction:

> Readers of the Authorized Version will immediately be struck by the absence of several pronouns: thee, thou, and ye are replaced by the simple you, while your and yours are substituted for thy and thine as applicable. Thee, thou, thy, and thine were once forms of address to express a special relationship to human as well as divine persons. These pronouns are no longer part of our language (New KJV).

This, of course, overlooks the fact that you is found hundreds of times in the AV. Along with ye it is used as a plural; while thee and thou are singular. Thus, by making you stand for both, the distinction between singular and plural in pronominal usage is lost in the modern versions. In some instances, the newer Bibles must resort to footnotes to clarify this. The translation in the commentaries of William Hendriksen has "you" for singular and "y o u" for plural, No wonder D.A. Carson admits:

> It Is true that Elizabethan English is more precise than modern English In its use of pronouns (The King James Version Debate, p. 98).

While thee and thou have not been used for many generations in common speech, they continued to be so used in addressing the Lord. As late as 1960 the presenters of the liberal New English Bible said:

> It was thought that the public for whom the N.E.B. was intended was not generally ready for the use of "you" in address to God, with all the overtones of familiarity and casual speech that this would bring with it ("Handbook to N.E.B." quoted in Trinitarian Bible Society Quarterly Record, date not known, p. 1).

It still has overtones of familiarity!

> ...critics of the use of thou, thee and thy insist that the ancient languages did not use a different form of the personal pronouns in speech addressed to God, This Is quite true, but when the Holy Scriptures are translated Into another language the translators have to take Into account all the phenomena of the receptor language...In this respect the English language has acquired, developed and retained a distinctive usage for all speech addressed to

God. (Ibid, p. 2,3).

Praise the Lord!

CONCLUSION

The material given in these twenty-one "biggest problem passages" is by no means complete or exhaustive. Others will be able to add further light.

But the above demonstrates how foolish and unfair it is to criticize passages such as these without taking the time to see If there is a reasonable explanation.

Some years ago, a NASA space probe gave the world its first close-up of the rings of Saturn. Prior to this the nature and structure of these rings were thought to be fairly straightforward. In fact, it was shown to be quite the opposite! Not only did the rings orbit Saturn, but the rings themselves contained orbiting "rings." They displayed a previously unimagined complexity. So it is with our English Bible. From a distance misapprehensions are possible. But the closer one looks, the more it reveals the hand of God. It bears witness to the fact that indeed it is the fulfillment of God's promise to preserve His original work of inspiration. Far from its "problem passages" revealing any deficiency; under scrutiny, these reveal "dust of gold" (Job 28:6). And what is more, they test the heart and motives of all who come to its pages!

Concerning thy testimonies, I have known of old that thou has founded them for ever. Psalms 119:152

ABOUT THE AUTHOR

Dr. J. A. Moorman, 2017

Dr. Jack Moorman went to his home in glory in 2021. We have lost a great student and scholar of the Scriptures. He is missed.

Jack A. Moorman studied for a while at the Indianapolis campus of Purdue University, attended briefly Indiana Bible College, and graduated from Tennessee Temple Bible School. He was with Baptist International Missions Inc. (BIMI) since 1967 and was involved in church planting, Bible Institute teaching and extensive distribution of Scriptures and gospel tracts in Johannesburg, South Africa from 1968–1988, and in England and London since 1988. He married his wife, Dot, on November 22, 1963.

J.A. Moorman has written the following scholarly books defending the King James Bible and the Hebrew, Aramaic and Greek words that underlie it:

When the KJV Departs from the "Majority" Text.

Early Manuscripts, Church Fathers, and the Authorized Version.

Forever Settled.

Missing in Modern Bibles—The Old Heresy Revived.

Samuel P. Tregelles—The Man Who Made the Critical Text Acceptable to Bible Believers.

8,000 Differences Between the Textus Receptus and the Critical Text.

Bible Chronology: The Two Great Divides.

The Biblical and Observational Case for Geocentricity.

These well-documented works are replete with evidence which he gleaned from his own resources as well as references found in the British Museum, British Library and other libraries in South Africa and the United Kingdom.

He was the pastor of Bethel Baptist Church in London, England since 1993. A great deal of his time, and on a nearly daily basis, was spent in distributing Gospel Literature on the crowded streets of London and beyond. May God bless his unfailing service to the Lord Jesus Christ.

Dr. Moorman has written many books and articles. Here are a few that are available through "The Old Paths Publications":

http://theoldpathspublications.com/Pages/BookStore.htm

1. Missing in Modern Bibles
2. Was Codex Sinaiticus Written In 1840?
3. Delivered from the Wrath to Come: A Study of the Pretribulational Rapture
4. Early Manuscripts, Church Fathers, and the Authorized Version
5. The Church, the Beginning, Baptism, Body, and Bride
6. The Biblical and Observational Case for Geocentricity
7. 8,000 Differences Between the N.T. Greek Words of the King James Bible and the Modern Versions
8. When the KJV Departs From the "Majority" Text
9. Bible Chronology - The Two Great Divides
10. Forever Settled, A Survey of the Document and History of the Bible
11. Genesis to the Exodus
12. Daniel: The Times of the Gentiles and the Times of Jerusalem
13. Revelation: God's Final Word

You may contact us by email:
TOP@theoldpathspublications.com

PAT@theoldpathspublications.com

H.D. Williams, M.D., Ph.D., President
The Old Paths Publications

www.ingramcontent.com/pod-product-compliance
Lightning Source LLC
LaVergne TN
LVHW020652100826
845148LV00012B/2453

* 9 7 8 1 7 3 7 6 3 8 4 2 1 *